This Book Belongs To

_____

Cryptogram #1

Each of these Cryptograms is a message in substitution code. THE SILLY DOG might become UJD WQPPZ BVN if U is substituted for T, J for H, D for E, etc. One way to break the code is to look for repeated letters. E, T, A, O, N, R and I are the most often used letters. A single letter is usually A or I; OF, IS and IT are common 2-letter words; try THE or AND for a 3-letter group. The code is different for each Cryptogram.

1. Ulom isxflos C xfqqkm oss cm, zkso qkm asfq C xfq qkm ispcsns cm!

2. Osouxvjx hn Gjqqzyooi kzu j gzuuzu kji, yo pfnb ez dujmx hi Zdbzlou.

3. Dxz sbft dxobr qz xyez ds kzyw ou kzyw oduzfk, ybm uaomzwu.

Cryptogram #2

Each of these Cryptograms is a message in substitution code. THE SILLY DOG might become UJD WQPPZ BVN if U is substituted for T, J for H, D for E, etc. One way to break the code is to look for repeated letters. E, T, A, O, N, R and I are the most often used letters. A single letter is usually A or I; OF, IS and IT are common 2-letter words; try THE or AND for a 3-letter group. The code is different for each Cryptogram.

1. Tvzvi pidmp ytepnrtc pnyp kyt pnrtj gbi rpmvag rg ebd kyt☐p mvv qnviv rp jvvfm rpm liyrt.

2. Pkquklk vifduvo wib dkjh, jve ivqw ivk djqg fdjf wib mkk.

3. Ugcb awspgcw Y spttrb cww yb, vrwc trb lwpt Y spt trb awxywfw yb!

Set up a glow-in-the-dark ring toss—use dollar-store glow necklaces or bracelets as rings.

What do I need to do this activity?

Notes

Cryptogram #3

Each of these Cryptograms is a message in substitution code. THE SILLY DOG might become UJD WQPPZ BVN if U is substituted for T, J for H, D for E, etc. One way to break the code is to look for repeated letters. E, T, A, O, N, R and I are the most often used letters. A single letter is usually A or I; OF, IS and IT are common 2-letter words; try THE or AND for a 3-letter group. The code is different for each Cryptogram.

1. Jytj sv fcj wdtw qysky ktf djdpftm msd.

2. X lw ac usly X sxqg xz l ocvsy ofgvg rfgvg lvg Circhgva.

3. Qtkzjt, lzht szjt gt jmvtf zybot!

Organize a massive water gun battle.

What do I need to do this activity?	Notes

Cryptogram #4

Each of these Cryptograms is a message in substitution code. THE SILLY DOG might become UJD WQPPZ BVN if U is substituted for T, J for H, D for E, etc. One way to break the code is to look for repeated letters. E, T, A, O, N, R and I are the most often used letters. A single letter is usually A or I; OF, IS and IT are common 2-letter words; try THE or AND for a 3-letter group. The code is different for each Cryptogram.

1. Ygcusky sx c qgswycouy ijcly ldyj cacdo woyjjo, cou bsdfjy kgdyrjl do qgj qljjy qgcq qsodagq dy Gcvvskjjo!

2. Qbwouo yjh qwakrjo lwxt uw nkyf wj ubt erjyk hyf we Wluwatm!

3. Vag bidugyfg df tbqq wt sozdpoq vadizf kovdgivqx hodvdiz twy wby hdvf vw zywh faoykgy.

Paint the sidewalk with water. See how fast the sun makes your art disappear.

What do I need to do this activity?	Notes

Cryptogram #5

Each of these Cryptograms is a message in substitution code. THE SILLY DOG might become UJD WQPPZ BVN if U is substituted for T, J for H, D for E, etc. One way to break the code is to look for repeated letters. E, T, A, O, N, R and I are the most often used letters. A single letter is usually A or I; OF, IS and IT are common 2-letter words; try THE or AND for a 3-letter group. The code is different for each Cryptogram.

1. B phon amia bs qnpntyiabse Mipphknns, kn qis ena phva bs amn riebq hd rijn-tnpbnon isw disaivc sh riaany kmia ien kn iyn!

2. Dxsltx, zlix vltx ux tjhxo lnwqx!

3. Kyl zynmkm dvl gds gxk kyl ntl kydk cm hxvmls cm kyl yldselmm ynvmlbdt.

Go geocaching, a fun high-tech scavenger hunt that you can do with a smartphone. You can play anywhere caches are hidden, but we have tips on how to start in Los Angeles, NYC, and New Jersey.

What do I need to do this activity?	Notes

Cryptogram #6

Each of these Cryptograms is a message in substitution code. THE SILLY DOG might become UJD WQPPZ BVN if U is substituted for T, J for H, D for E, etc. One way to break the code is to look for repeated letters. E, T, A, O, N, R and I are the most often used letters. A single letter is usually A or I; OF, IS and IT are common 2-letter words; try THE or AND for a 3-letter group. The code is different for each Cryptogram.

1. B ivrno qn zoeop nwqcc qz abpdzonn wv wivno yiv cqnwoz qzwozwcm; bz rzobpwicm ibza kponnon wio nzqf vu wio yqzavy, wio cbwgi pqnon.

2. Dlnepe ixr dncykxe znwj pn gyis nx plj vkxiy ris nv Nzpncjm!

3. R fg jc mnfo R nrqs rk f vcpno vusps lusps fps Cblchspj.

Get some pots and pans for drums, dress up and have a parade.

What do I need to do this activity?	Notes

Cryptogram #7

Each of these Cryptograms is a message in substitution code. THE SILLY DOG might become UJD WQPPZ BVN if U is substituted for T, J for H, D for E, etc. One way to break the code is to look for repeated letters. E, T, A, O, N, R and I are the most often used letters. A single letter is usually A or I; OF, IS and IT are common 2-letter words; try THE or AND for a 3-letter group. The code is different for each Cryptogram.

1. Mifqhq vey mfrkjeq tfcn hf akvw fe hin zjevk yvw fz Fthfrnd!

2. Dnxbnhn zikgbzl piq gnof, ozt izxp izn goxa kgok piq enn.

3. D tr bu svtq D vdkn dl t muovq menon henon ton Uwhuxnob.

Color Me In

Cryptogram #8

Each of these Cryptograms is a message in substitution code. THE SILLY DOG might become UJD WQPPZ BVN if U is substituted for T, J for H, D for E, etc. One way to break the code is to look for repeated letters. E, T, A, O, N, R and I are the most often used letters. A single letter is usually A or I; OF, IS and IT are common 2-letter words; try THE or AND for a 3-letter group. The code is different for each Cryptogram.

1. Rk rf gmfk h cmavu ye uyvmf zyvmf!

2. Gnrzvn, yzjn szvn mn vwanq zkdin!

3. Wypyl dlgrd jwkdqbwa dqjd ijw dqbwt uxl bdrysu bu kxg ijw☐d ryy cqyly bd tyyhr bdr mljbw.

Go on an alphabet treasure hunt. See if you can find things that begin with every letter in nature.

What do I need to do this activity?	Notes

Cryptogram #9

Each of these Cryptograms is a message in substitution code. THE SILLY DOG might become UJD WQPPZ BVN if U is substituted for T, J for H, D for E, etc. One way to break the code is to look for repeated letters. E, T, A, O, N, R and I are the most often used letters. A single letter is usually A or I; OF, IS and IT are common 2-letter words; try THE or AND for a 3-letter group. The code is different for each Cryptogram.

1. Dh bcwbtq. Dh mhwg bcwbtq.

2. Ha hd qgda k xgrwt up tuwgd muwgd!

3. Nzq rkseqfhq sh brvv jb gxwsdxv nzskwh uxnsqknva lxsnskw bjf jrf lsnh nj wfjl hzxfuqf.

Create a short stop-motion film using dolls, stuffed animals or action figures. There are lots of apps that make this easy.

What do I need to do this activity?	Notes

Cryptogram #10

Each of these Cryptograms is a message in substitution code. THE SILLY DOG might become UJD WQPPZ BVN if U is substituted for T, J for H, D for E, etc. One way to break the code is to look for repeated letters. E, T, A, O, N, R and I are the most often used letters. A single letter is usually A or I; OF, IS and IT are common 2-letter words; try THE or AND for a 3-letter group. The code is different for each Cryptogram.

1. Itw paiy chwi l ndyynw slk ihswydswi. Bw lnn ch l ndyynw slk ihswydswi.

2. Ewa swnyey gma hgt hxe ewa nka ewge jy zxmyat jy ewa wagtqayy wnmyargk.

3. W ngxa raau aukcbn nkvvkv qkxwar sk eukj sngs guh jawvfk jagvwub g qgre wr uaxav mvwaufyh.

Color Me In

Cryptogram #11

Each of these Cryptograms is a message in substitution code. THE SILLY DOG might become UJD WQPPZ BVN if U is substituted for T, J for H, D for E, etc. One way to break the code is to look for repeated letters. E, T, A, O, N, R and I are the most often used letters. A single letter is usually A or I; OF, IS and IT are common 2-letter words; try THE or AND for a 3-letter group. The code is different for each Cryptogram.

1. Ynqoq jnqoq vr sb vauxvsujvbs, jnqoq vr sb nboobo.

2. Rkv tnrd chvr s yuddyv jsg rhjvdujvr. Ov syy ch s yuddyv jsg rhjvdujvr.

3. Uahlf lptcjv hq yjqnve pyattjnar.

Put a small toy in a balloon, fill it with water and freeze. You'll end up with a toy frozen in a big chunk of ice.

What do I need to do this activity?	Notes

Cryptogram #12

Each of these Cryptograms is a message in substitution code. THE SILLY DOG might become UJD WQPPZ BVN if U is substituted for T, J for H, D for E, etc. One way to break the code is to look for repeated letters. E, T, A, O, N, R and I are the most often used letters. A single letter is usually A or I; OF, IS and IT are common 2-letter words; try THE or AND for a 3-letter group. The code is different for each Cryptogram.

1. E sw ng jvsr E vedf el s kgbvr kifbf qifbf sbf Gtqghfbn.

2. Hcuce fegif bhxfqrhk fqbf nbh fqrhv yje rficay ry xjg nbh☐f icc lqcec rf vccoi rfi tebrh.

3. Qo qz gbzo m sbhfj ck jcfbz icfbz!

Color Me In

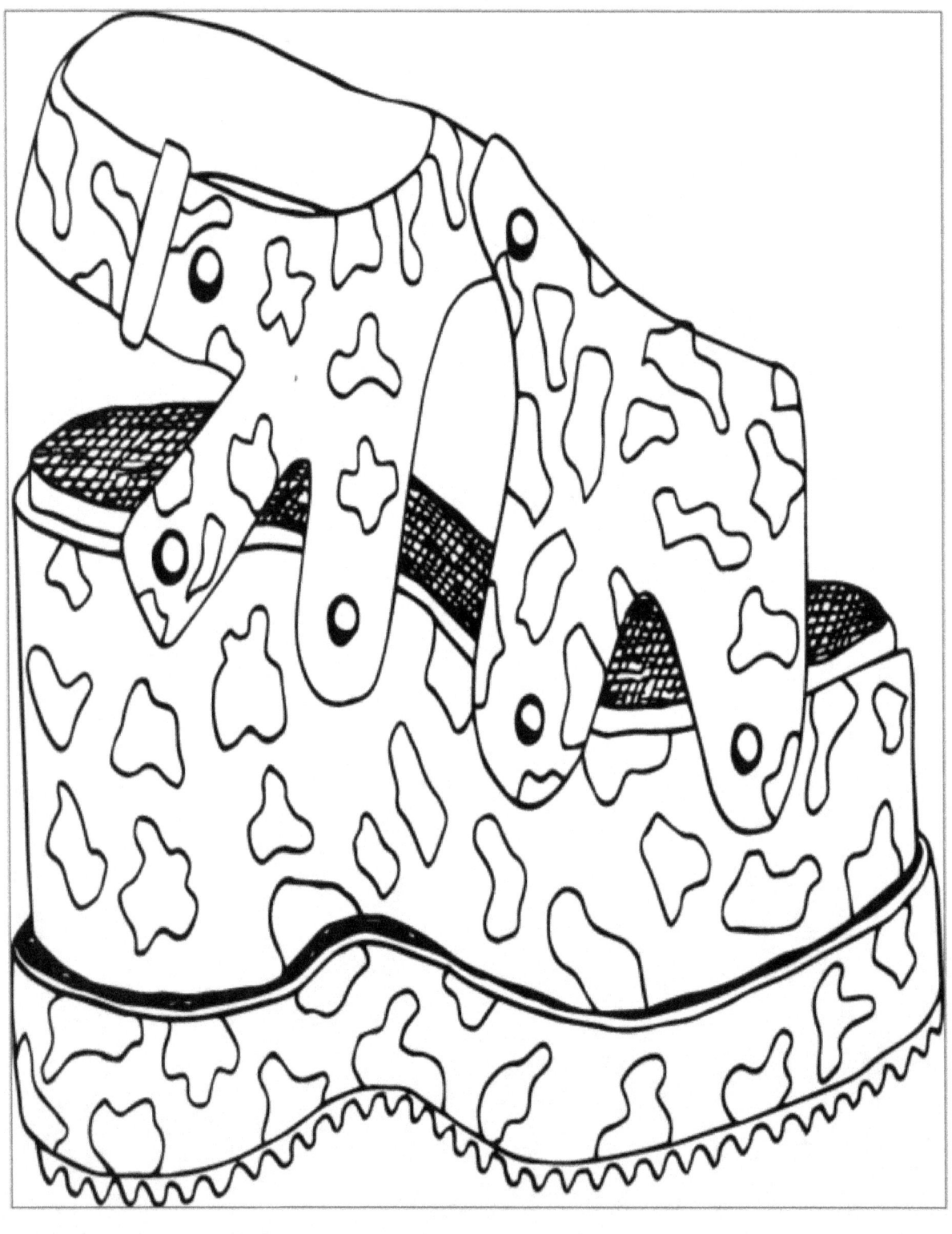

Cryptogram #13

Each of these Cryptograms is a message in substitution code. THE SILLY DOG might become UJD WQPPZ BVN if U is substituted for T, J for H, D for E, etc. One way to break the code is to look for repeated letters. E, T, A, O, N, R and I are the most often used letters. A single letter is usually A or I; OF, IS and IT are common 2-letter words; try THE or AND for a 3-letter group. The code is different for each Cryptogram.

1. Jm igd hvxtoxkb al nm igqnje, eandigxkb sxtodw igxe sfm tande.

2. Qw vws xouj xj pjs sij ehlgvp xwvujlb.

3. N bxcyl dy tlrlz ysdhh dt inzatlyy sx sbxyl jbx hdyslt dtsltshe; nt ctlnzsbhe bnti fzlyyly sbl ytdm xk sbl jdtixj, sbl hnsvb zdyly.

Have a bird-call imitation contest. See who can do the best owl screech, blue jay squawk or chickadee tweet.

What do I need to do this activity?	Notes

Cryptogram #14

Each of these Cryptograms is a message in substitution code. THE SILLY DOG might become UJD WQPPZ BVN if U is substituted for T, J for H, D for E, etc. One way to break the code is to look for repeated letters. E, T, A, O, N, R and I are the most often used letters. A single letter is usually A or I; OF, IS and IT are common 2-letter words; try THE or AND for a 3-letter group. The code is different for each Cryptogram.

1. Fts nubcswqs bq inoo ji gzabpzo ftbuaq xzfbsufok hzbfbua ijw jnw hbfq fj awjh qtzwxsw.

2. E rafyw by pwuwh yvbxx bp zehopwyy va vrayw dra xbyvwp bpvwpvxm; ep fpwehvrxm repz shwyywy vrw ypbj ag vrw dbpzad, vrw xevqr hbywy.

3. Df wzx scyqeylo ba kf wzhkdr, rbkxwzylo uyqext wzyr umf qbkxr.

Stage a massive bubble battle and invite the whole block.

What do I need to do this activity?	Notes

Cryptogram #15

Each of these Cryptograms is a message in substitution code. THE SILLY DOG might become UJD WQPPZ BVN if U is substituted for T, J for H, D for E, etc. One way to break the code is to look for repeated letters. E, T, A, O, N, R and I are the most often used letters. A single letter is usually A or I; OF, IS and IT are common 2-letter words; try THE or AND for a 3-letter group. The code is different for each Cryptogram.

1. Yc seqskh. Yc ucqf seqskh.

2. Pubcdfp dh b gudvpblcp trbep expr bwbxl vlprrl, blc ndxorp fuxpjre xl gur gerrp gubg gdlxwug xp Ubkkdfrrl!

3. Gdur sgda, frg Hagdf Cpxcbwl awkgk ypf ye frg cpxcbwl cdfr frdf rg frwlbk wk frg xykf kwlugag.

Color Me In

Cryptogram #16

Each of these Cryptograms is a message in substitution code. THE SILLY DOG might become UJD WQPPZ BVN if U is substituted for T, J for H, D for E, etc. One way to break the code is to look for repeated letters. E, T, A, O, N, R and I are the most often used letters. A single letter is usually A or I; OF, IS and IT are common 2-letter words; try THE or AND for a 3-letter group. The code is different for each Cryptogram.

1. Ukgu yz rmu eqge vkyik igr quqfrgh hyq.

2. F kgxp wqhw fs vpkpauhwfst Qhkkgepps, ep vhs tpw kgbw fs wqp rhtfv gn rhmp-apkfpxp hsz nhswhbl sg rhwwpu eqhw htp ep hup!

3. Jwbshw, yscw ushw zw hgiwt svpaw!

Learn how to do yo-yo tricks.

What do I need to do this activity?	Notes

Cryptogram #17

Each of these Cryptograms is a message in substitution code. THE SILLY DOG might become UJD WQPPZ BVN if U is substituted for T, J for H, D for E, etc. One way to break the code is to look for repeated letters. E, T, A, O, N, R and I are the most often used letters. A single letter is usually A or I; OF, IS and IT are common 2-letter words; try THE or AND for a 3-letter group. The code is different for each Cryptogram.

1. Etxrot, vrut zrot ft oqyta rslgt!

2. Fywqyoy hxdrqhc lxi rysa, shj xhwl xhy rswb drsd lxi myy.

3. Kogk dw rzk cfgc bodno ngr fkfxrgu udf.

Organize a family game night and pull out old standards like Monopoly, Scrabble and Pictionary. Winners can earn points to cash in for small prizes or extra scoops of ice cream.

What do I need to do this activity?	Notes

Cryptogram #18

Each of these Cryptograms is a message in substitution code. THE SILLY DOG might become UJD WQPPZ BVN if U is substituted for T, J for H, D for E, etc. One way to break the code is to look for repeated letters. E, T, A, O, N, R and I are the most often used letters. A single letter is usually A or I; OF, IS and IT are common 2-letter words; try THE or AND for a 3-letter group. The code is different for each Cryptogram.

1. Itrdr qtrdr wj sc whpxwspqwcs, qtrdr wj sc tcddcd.

2. L pqho dooc ocetzp peyyey jehlod ie ucer ipqi qck rolywe roqylcz q jqdu ld cohoy aylocwfk.

3. Slkrlwl hdpzrhb tdy zlgu, ghv dhkt dhl zgko pzgp tdy mll.

Color Me In

Cryptogram #19

Each of these Cryptograms is a message in substitution code. THE SILLY DOG might become UJD WQPPZ BVN if U is substituted for T, J for H, D for E, etc. One way to break the code is to look for repeated letters. E, T, A, O, N, R and I are the most often used letters. A single letter is usually A or I; OF, IS and IT are common 2-letter words; try THE or AND for a 3-letter group. The code is different for each Cryptogram.

1. Rk nqt liebgemo jp dk nqzdrx,
   xjdtnqemo hebgtv nqex hck bjdtx.

2. Buwypz, buwypz, guap teb gcuwypz.
   Iacz ywce teb dtwpbcue ywyypz.

3. T okxz ygly tm nzozdvlytmi
   Glookfzzm, fz nlm izy okhy tm ygz
   ulitn kb ulpz-dzotzxz lme blmylhs mk
   ulyyzv fgly liz fz lvz!

See who can create the best shadow figures. All you need is a flashlight, a sheet and your hands.

What do I need to do this activity?	Notes

Cryptogram #20

Each of these Cryptograms is a message in substitution code. THE SILLY DOG might become UJD WQPPZ BVN if U is substituted for T, J for H, D for E, etc. One way to break the code is to look for repeated letters. E, T, A, O, N, R and I are the most often used letters. A single letter is usually A or I; OF, IS and IT are common 2-letter words; try THE or AND for a 3-letter group. The code is different for each Cryptogram.

1. Yautqt nrc yulwjrt kuhz qu fwno ur qaz pjrnw cno up Ukqulzd!

2. Fb Whnnfkrrb, ksumwrp mfcr ugdr; ksnt lwfpup rpmhor xgfc tgrhcp. Rhmw cfbpurg thbmrp sb uwr ohgy.

3. Vpgv dk ibv cogc hpdep egi ovoqigx xdo.

Cryptogram #21

Each of these Cryptograms is a message in substitution code. THE SILLY DOG might become UJD WQPPZ BVN if U is substituted for T, J for H, D for E, etc. One way to break the code is to look for repeated letters. E, T, A, O, N, R and I are the most often used letters. A single letter is usually A or I; OF, IS and IT are common 2-letter words; try THE or AND for a 3-letter group. The code is different for each Cryptogram.

1. K xjad pddm dmrtlx xryyry crakdp gr nmrq gxjg jms qdkywr qdjykml j cjpn kp mdady iykdmwvs.

2. Fvowatf ar o ivayfouwf bpoxf xqfp odoqu yufppu, ouw laqjpf tvqfepx qu ivp ixppf ivoi iauqdvi qf Vokkatppu!

3. Uqunbsyb ez Xyvvwmuul cwn y xwnnwn cyl, mu idzk ow jnypb el Wjkwrun.

Cryptogram #22

Each of these Cryptograms is a message in substitution code. THE SILLY DOG might become UJD WQPPZ BVN if U is substituted for T, J for H, D for E, etc. One way to break the code is to look for repeated letters. E, T, A, O, N, R and I are the most often used letters. A single letter is usually A or I; OF, IS and IT are common 2-letter words; try THE or AND for a 3-letter group. The code is different for each Cryptogram.

1. Vyzt rvye, stv Wevys Jlxjhbo ebivi uls ua stv jlxjhbo jyst stys tv stbohi bi stv xuis ibozvev.

2. Fzuze iepwi ofkibsfr iboi nof ibsfd gle siwzxg sg klp nof□i wzz hbzez si dzzjw siw meosf.

3. Lthuit, funt puit xt iegtb urzat!

Cryptogram #23

Each of these Cryptograms is a message in substitution code. THE SILLY DOG might become UJD WQPPZ BVN if U is substituted for T, J for H, D for E, etc. One way to break the code is to look for repeated letters. E, T, A, O, N, R and I are the most often used letters. A single letter is usually A or I; OF, IS and IT are common 2-letter words; try THE or AND for a 3-letter group. The code is different for each Cryptogram.

1. Lapl qt zdl kgpk saqea epz glgmzpr rqg.

2. Cbhn dvgybhv J gyaarn hvv jn, mrvh arn xvya J gya arn dvwjvzv jn!

3. Kgpfbf lhr kpzuehf ipcj bp vulm ph bgj dehlu rlm pd Pibpzjw!

Cryptogram #24

Each of these Cryptograms is a message in substitution code. THE SILLY DOG might become UJD WQPPZ BVN if U is substituted for T, J for H, D for E, etc. One way to break the code is to look for repeated letters. E, T, A, O, N, R and I are the most often used letters. A single letter is usually A or I; OF, IS and IT are common 2-letter words; try THE or AND for a 3-letter group. The code is different for each Cryptogram.

1. Bwys jbwf, dsb Mfbwd Eoceuth ftnbn xod xr dsb eoceuth ewds dswd sb dsthun tn dsb cxnd nthybfb.

2. Hgmgq rqier yhkrnfhu rnyr wyh rnfhj xbq fregpx fx kbi wyh☐r egg lngqg fr jggte fre vqyfh.

3. Cymtyly wpbatws rpz aydq, dwe pwmr pwy admn badb rpz fyy.

Cryptogram #25

Each of these Cryptograms is a message in substitution code. THE SILLY DOG might become UJD WQPPZ BVN if U is substituted for T, J for H, D for E, etc. One way to break the code is to look for repeated letters. E, T, A, O, N, R and I are the most often used letters. A single letter is usually A or I; OF, IS and IT are common 2-letter words; try THE or AND for a 3-letter group. The code is different for each Cryptogram.

1. Fdvl mfdp, clf Bpfdc Xznxato ptufu rzc rs clf xznxato xdcl cldc lf cltoau tu clf nruc utovfpf.

2. Pd Ufaapykkd, ymojukt jpwk oxek; ymal suptot ktjfck zxpw lxkfwt. Kfju wpdtokx lfdjkt md ouk cfxv.

3. Uv xroxne. Uv cvoz xroxne.

Cryptogram #26

Each of these Cryptograms is a message in substitution code. THE SILLY DOG might become UJD WQPPZ BVN if U is substituted for T, J for H, D for E, etc. One way to break the code is to look for repeated letters. E, T, A, O, N, R and I are the most often used letters. A single letter is usually A or I; OF, IS and IT are common 2-letter words; try THE or AND for a 3-letter group. The code is different for each Cryptogram.

1. Tq Mwjjtvbbq, vfkombi otrb kdcb; vfjn hmtiki biowyb pdtr ndbwri. Bwom rtqikbd nwqobi fq kmb ywds.

2. C tgon yvby ck dntnrfbyckm Vbttginnk, in dbk mny tgly ck yvn abmcd gz abwn-rntcnon bku zbkyblh kg abyynf ivby bmn in bfn!

3. Nlftab, nlftab, plda qhn pmlftab. Odmb tfmh qhn gqfanmlh tfttab.

Cryptogram #27

Each of these Cryptograms is a message in substitution code. THE SILLY DOG might become UJD WQPPZ BVN if U is substituted for T, J for H, D for E, etc. One way to break the code is to look for repeated letters. E, T, A, O, N, R and I are the most often used letters. A single letter is usually A or I; OF, IS and IT are common 2-letter words; try THE or AND for a 3-letter group. The code is different for each Cryptogram.

1. Us uw ryws g oymxa tj atxyw etxyw!

2. Soks ep tjs rckr noevo vkt cscwtkh hec.

3. Dk obhogn. Dk qkhu obhogn.

Cryptogram #28

Each of these Cryptograms is a message in substitution code. THE SILLY DOG might become UJD WQPPZ BVN if U is substituted for T, J for H, D for E, etc. One way to break the code is to look for repeated letters. E, T, A, O, N, R and I are the most often used letters. A single letter is usually A or I; OF, IS and IT are common 2-letter words; try THE or AND for a 3-letter group. The code is different for each Cryptogram.

1. Apakgwcg qm Tczzhlaad jhk c thkkhk jcd, la oemv uh ikcbg qd Hivhxak.

2. Thpqmx, thpqmx, bhsm krt bfhpqmx. Usfx qpfr krt dkpmtfhr qpqqmx.

3. Xojybo, sywo pybo zo bkmof yalqo!

Cryptogram #29

Each of these Cryptograms is a message in substitution code. THE SILLY DOG might become UJD WQPPZ BVN if U is substituted for T, J for H, D for E, etc. One way to break the code is to look for repeated letters. E, T, A, O, N, R and I are the most often used letters. A single letter is usually A or I; OF, IS and IT are common 2-letter words; try THE or AND for a 3-letter group. The code is different for each Cryptogram.

1. Uah bapeue zgh szj sfu uah pwh uazu ke tfgehj ke uah ahzjyhee apgehlzw.

2. Zxtdt lxtdt ag mh afwiamwlahm, lxtdt ag mh xhddhd.

3. Jkdj qa ztj wndw lkquk udz njnbzdo oqn.

Cryptogram #30

Each of these Cryptograms is a message in substitution code. THE SILLY DOG might become UJD WQPPZ BVN if U is substituted for T, J for H, D for E, etc. One way to break the code is to look for repeated letters. E, T, A, O, N, R and I are the most often used letters. A single letter is usually A or I; OF, IS and IT are common 2-letter words; try THE or AND for a 3-letter group. The code is different for each Cryptogram.

1. Ejxmx gjxmx uy cf urdzucdgufc, gjxmx uy cf jfmmfm.

2. Lp Nxfflarrp, askvnrh vlgr kqcr; asfw dnlhkh rhvxzr jqlg wqrxgh. Rxvn glphkrq wxpvrh sp knr zxqt.

3. Ur sypske. Ur brpx sypske.

Answer Key

Cryptogram #1
From Page 5

1. Ulom isxtlos C xtqqkm oss cm, zkso qkm asfq C xfq qkm ispcsns cm!

   Just because I cannot see it, does not mean I can not believe it!

2. Osouxvjx hn Gjqqzyooi kzu j gzuuzu kji, yo pfnb ez dujmx hi Zdbzlou.

   Everyday is Halloween for a horror fan, we just go crazy in October.

3. Dxz sbft dxobr qz xyez ds kzyw ou kzyw oduzfk, ybm uaomzwu.

   The only thing we have to fear is fear itself, and spiders.

Cryptogram #2
From Page 7

1. Tvzvi pidmp ytepnrtc pnyp kyt pnrtj gbi rpmvag rg ebd kyt'p mvv qnviv rp jvvfm rpm liyrt.

   Never trust anything that can think for itself if you can't see where it keeps its brain.

2. Pkquklk vifduvo wib dkjh, jve ivqw ivk djqg fdjf wib mkk.

   Believe nothing you hear, and only one half that you see.

3. Ugcb awspgcw Y spttrb cww yb, vrwc trb lwpt Y spt trb awxywfw yb!

   Just because I cannot see it, does not mean I can not believe it!

Cryptogram #3
From Page 9

1. Jytj sv tcj wdtw qysky ktt djdpttm msd.

   That is not dead which can eternal lie.

2. X lw ac usly X sxqg xz l ocvsy ofgvg rfgvg lvg Circhgva.

   I am so glad I live in a world where there are Octobers.

3. Qtkzjt, lzht szjt gt jmvtf zybot!

   Beware, take care he rides alone!

Cryptogram #4
From Page 11

1. Ygcusky sx c qgswycouy ijcly ldyj cacdo woyjjo, cou bsdfjy kgdyrjl do qgj qljjy qgcq qsodagq dy Gcvvskjjo!

   Shadows of a thousands years rise again unseen, and voices whisper in the trees that tonight is Halloween!

2. Qbwouo yjh qwakrjo lwxt uw nkyf wj ubt erjyk hyf we Wluwatm!

   Ghosts and goblins come to play on the final day of October!

3. Vag bidugyfg df tbqq wt sozdpoq vadizf kovdgivqx hodvdiz twy wby hdvf vw zywh faoykgy.

   The universe is full of magical things patiently waiting for our wits to grow sharper.

Cryptogram #5
From Page 13

1. B phon amia bs qnpntyiabse
   Mipphknns, kn qis ena phva bs amn
   riebq hd rijn-tnpbnon isw disaivc sh
   riaany kmia ien kn iyn!

   > I love that in celebrating Halloween, we can get lost in the magic of make-believe and fantasy no matter what age we are!

2. Dxsltx, zlix vltx ux tjhxo lnwqx!

   > Beware, take care he rides alone!

3. Kyl zynmkm dvl gds gxk kyl ntl kydk
   cm hxvmls cm kyl yldselmm ynvmlbdt.

   > The ghosts are bad but the one that is cursed is the headless horseman.

Cryptogram #6
From Page 15

1. B ivrno qn zoeop nwqcc qz abpdzonn
   wv wivno yiv cqnwoz qzwozwcm; bz
   rzobpwicm ibza kponnon wio nzqf vu
   wio yqzavy, wio cbwgi pqnon.

   > A house is never still in darkness to those who listen intently; an unearthly hand presses the snib of the window, the latch rises.

2. Dlnepe ixr dncykxe znwj pn gyis nx
   plj vkxiy ris nv Nzpncjm!

   > Ghosts and goblins come to play on the final day of October!

3. R fg jc mnfo R nrqs rk f vcpno vusps
   lusps fps Cblchspj.

   > I am so glad I live in a world where there are Octobers.

Cryptogram #7
From Page 17

1. Mitqhq vey mtrkjeq ttcn ht akvw te
   hin zjevk yvw fz Fthfrnd!

   > Ghosts and goblins come to play on the final day of October!

2. Dnxbnhn zikgbzl piq gnof, ozt izxp
   izn goxa kgok piq enn.

   > Believe nothing you hear, and only one half that you see.

3. D tr bu svtq D vdkn dl t muovq menon
   henon ton Uwhuxnob.

   > I am so glad I live in a world where there are Octobers.

Cryptogram #8
From Page 19

1. Rk rt gmtk h cmavu ye uyvmt zyvmt!

   > It is just a bunch of hocus pocus!

2. Gnrzvn, yzjn szvn mn vwanq zkdin!

   > Beware, take care he rides alone!

3. Wypyl dlgrd jwkdqbwa dqjd ijw dqbwt
   uxl bdrysu bu kxg ijw d ryy
   cqyly bd tyyhr bdr mljbw.

   > Never trust anything that can think for itself if you can't see where it keeps its brain.

Cryptogram #9
From Page 21

1. Dh bcwbtq. Dh mhwg bcwbtq.
   > Be afraid. Be very afraid.

2. Ha hd qgda k xgrwt up tuwgd muwgd!
   > It is just a bunch of hocus pocus!

3. Nzq rkseqfhq sh brvv jb gxwsdxv nzskwh uxnsqknva lxsnskw bjf jrf lsnh nj wfjl hzxfuqf.
   > The universe is full of magical things patiently waiting for our wits to grow sharper.

Cryptogram #10
From Page 23

1. Itw paiy chwi l ndyynw slk ihswydswi. Bw lnn ch l ndyynw slk ihswydswi.
   > She just goes a little mad sometimes. We all go a little mad sometimes.

2. Ewa swnyey gma hgt hxe ewa nka ewge jy zxmyat jy ewa wagtqayy wnmyargk.
   > The ghosts are bad but the one that is cursed is the headless horseman.

3. W ngxa raau aukcbn nkvvkv qkxwar sk eukj sngs guh jawvfk jagvwub g qgre wr uaxav mvwaufyh.
   > I have seen enough horror movies to know that any weirdo wearing a mask is never friendly.

Cryptogram #11
From Page 25

1. Ynqoq jnqoq vr sb vauxvsujvbs, jnqoq vr sb nboobo.
   > Where there is no imagination, there is no horror.

2. Rkv tnrd chvr s yuddyv jsg rhjvdujvr. Ov syy ch s yuddyv jsg rhjvdujvr.
   > She just goes a little mad sometimes. We all go a little mad sometimes.

3. Uahlf lptcjv hq yjqnve pyattjnar.
   > Being normal is vastly overrated.

Cryptogram #12
From Page 27

1. E sw ng jvsr E vedt el s kgbvr kitbt qifbf sbf Gtqghfbn.
   > I am so glad I live in a world where there are Octobers.

2. Hcuce fegif bhxfqrhk fqbf nbh fqrhv yje rficay ry xjg nbh f icc lqcec rf vccoi rfi tebrh.
   > Never trust anything that can think for itself if you can't see where it keeps its brain.

3. Qo qz gbzo m sbhfj ck jcfbz icfbz!
   > It is just a bunch of hocus pocus!

Cryptogram #13
From Page 29

1. Jm igd hvxtoxkb al nm igqnje,
   eandigxkb sxtodw igxe sfm tande.

   > By the pricking of my thumbs, something wicked
   > this way comes.

2. Qw vws xouj xj pjs sij ehlgvp
   xwvujlb.

   > Do not make me get the flying monkeys.

3. N bxcyl dy tlrlz ysdhh dt inzatlyy
   sx sbxyl jbx hdyslt dtsltshe; nt
   ctlnzsbhe bnti fzlyyly sbl ytdm xk
   sbl jdtixj, sbl hnsvb zdyly.

   > A house is never still in darkness to those who
   > listen intently; an unearthly hand presses the
   > snib of the window, the latch rises.

Cryptogram #14
From Page 31

1. Fts nubcswqs bq inoo ji gzabpzo
   ftbuaq xzfbsufok hzbfbua ijw jnw
   hbfq fj awjh qtzwxsw.

   > The universe is full of magical things patiently
   > waiting for our wits to grow sharper.

2. E rafyw by pwuwh yvbxx bp zehopwyy
   va vrayw dra xbyvwp bpvwpvxm; ep
   fpwehvrxm repz shwyywy vrw ypbj ag
   vrw dbpzad, vrw xevqr hbywy.

   > A house is never still in darkness to those who
   > listen intently; an unearthly hand presses the
   > snib of the window, the latch rises.

3. Df wzx scyqeylo ba kf wzhkdr,
   rbkxwzylo uyqext wzyr umf qbkxr.

   > By the pricking of my thumbs, something wicked
   > this way comes.

Cryptogram #15
From Page 33

1. Yc seqskh. Yc ucqt seqskh.

   > Be afraid. Be very afraid.

2. Pubcdfp dh b gudvpblcp trbep expr
   bwbxl vlprrl, blc ndxorp fuxpjre xl
   gur gerrp gubg gdlxwug xp Ubkkdfrrl!

   > Shadows of a thousands years rise again unseen,
   > and voices whisper in the trees that tonight is
   > Halloween!

3. Gdur sgda, frg Hagdf Cpxcbwl awkgk
   ypf ye frg cpxcbwl cdfr frdf rg
   frwlbk wk frg xykf kwlugag.

   > Each year, the Great Pumpkin rises out of the
   > pumpkin path that he thinks is the most sincere.

Cryptogram #16
From Page 35

1. Ukgu yz rmu eqge vkyik igr quqtrgh
   hyq.

   > That is not dead which can eternal lie.

2. F kgxp wqhw fs vpkpauhwfst
   Qhkkgepps, ep vhs tpw kgbw fs wqp
   rhtfv gn rhmp-apkfpxp hsz nhswhbl sg
   rhwwpu eqhw htp ep hup!

   > I love that in celebrating Halloween, we can get
   > lost in the magic of make-believe and fantasy no
   > matter what age we are!

3. Jwbshw, yscw ushw zw hgiwt svpaw!

   > Beware, take care he rides alone!

Cryptogram #17
From Page 37

1. Etxrot, vrut zrot tt oqyta rslgt!

   Beware, take care he rides alone!

2. Fywqyoy hxdrqhc lxi rysa, shj xhwl xhy rswb drsd lxi myy.

   Believe nothing you hear, and only one half that you see.

3. Kogk dw rzk cfgc bodno ngr fkfxrgu udf.

   That is not dead which can eternal lie.

Cryptogram #18
From Page 39

1. Itrdr qtrdr wj sc whpxwspqwcs, qtrdr wj sc tcddcd.

   Where there is no imagination, there is no horror.

2. L pqho dooc ocetzp peyyey jehlod ie ucer ipqi qck rolywe roqylcz q jqdu ld cohoy aylocwfk.

   I have seen enough horror movies to know that any weirdo wearing a mask is never friendly.

3. Slkrlwl hdpzrhb tdy zlgu, ghv dhkt dhl zgko pzgp tdy mll.

   Believe nothing you hear, and only one half that you see.

Cryptogram #19
From Page 41

1. Rk nqt liebgemo jp dk nqzdrx, xjdtnqemo hebgtv nqex hck bjdtx.

   By the pricking of my thumbs, something wicked this way comes.

2. Buwypz, buwypz, guap teb gcuwypz. Iacz ywce teb dtwpbcue ywyypz.

   Double, double, toil and trouble. Fire burn and cauldron bubble.

3. T okxz ygly tm nzozdvlytmi Gloockfzzm, fz nlm izy okhy tm ygz ulitn kb ulpz-dzotzxz lme blmylhs mk ulyyzv fgly liz fz lvz!

   I love that in celebrating Halloween, we can get lost in the magic of make-believe and fantasy no matter what age we are!

Cryptogram #20
From Page 43

1. Yautqt nrc yulwjrt kuhz qu twno ur qaz pjrnw cno up Ukqulzd!

   Ghosts and goblins come to play on the final day of October!

2. Fb Whnnfkrrb, ksumwrp mfcr ugdr; ksnt lwfpup rpmhor xgfc tgrhcp. Rhmw cfbpurg thbmrp sb uwr ohgy.

   On Halloween, witches come true; wild ghosts escape from dreams. Each monster dances in the park.

3. Vpgv dk ibv cogc hpdep egi ovoqigx xdo.

   That is not dead which can eternal lie.

Cryptogram #21
From Page 44

1. K xjad pddm dmrtlx xryyry crakdp gr nmrq gxjg jms qdkywr qdjykml j cjpn kp mdady iykdmwvs.

   I have seen enough horror movies to know that any weirdo wearing a mask is never friendly.

2. Fvowatf ar o ivayfouwf bpoxf xqfp odoqu yufppu, ouw laqjpf tvqfepx qu ivp ixppf ivoi iauqdvi qf Vokkatppu!

   Shadows of a thousands years rise again unseen, and voices whisper in the trees that tonight is Halloween!

3. Uqunbsyb ez Xyvvwmuul cwn y xwnnwn cyl, mu idzk ow jnypb el Wjkwrun.

   Everyday is Halloween for a horror fan, we just go crazy in October.

Cryptogram #22
From Page 45

1. Vyzt rvye, stv Wevys Jlxjhbo ebivi uls ua stv jlxjhbo jyst stys tv stbohi bi stv xuis ibozvev.

   Each year, the Great Pumpkin rises out of the pumpkin path that he thinks is the most sincere.

2. Fzuze iepwi ofkibsfr iboi nof ibsfd gle siwzxg sg klp nof i wzz hbzez si dzzjw siw meosf.

   Never trust anything that can think for itself if you can't see where it keeps its brain.

3. Lthuit, funt puit xt iegtb urzat!

   Beware, take care he rides alone!

Cryptogram #23
From Page 46

1. Lapl qt zdl kgpk saqea epz glgmzpr rqg.

   That is not dead which can eternal lie.

2. Cbhn dvgybhv J gyaarn hvv jn, mrvh arn xvya J gya arn dvwjvzv jn!

   Just because I cannot see it, does not mean I can not believe it!

3. Kgpfbf lhr kpzuehf ipcj bp vulm ph bgj dehlu rlm pd Pibpzjw!

   Ghosts and goblins come to play on the final day of October!

Cryptogram #24
From Page 47

1. Bwys jbwt, dsb Mtbwd Eoceuth ttnbn xod xr dsb eoceuth ewds dswd sb dsthun tn dsb cxnd nthybfb.

   Each year, the Great Pumpkin rises out of the pumpkin path that he thinks is the most sincere.

2. Hgmgq rqier yhkrnfhu rnyr wyh rnfhj xbq fregpx fx kbi wyh r egg lngqg fr jggte fre vqyfh.

   Never trust anything that can think for itself if you can't see where it keeps its brain.

3. Cymtyly wpbatws rpz aydq, dwe pwmr pwy admn badb rpz fyy.

   Believe nothing you hear, and only one half that you see.

Cryptogram #25
From Page 48

1. Fdvl mtdp, clt Bptdc Xznxato ptutu rzc rs clf xznxato xdcl cldc lf cltoau tu clf nruc utovfpf.

    Each year, the Great Pumpkin rises out of the pumpkin path that he thinks is the most sincere.

2. Pd Ufaapykkd, ymojukt jpwk oxek; ymal suptot ktjfck zxpw lxkfwt. Kfju wpdtokx lfdjkt md ouk cfxv.

    On Halloween, witches come true; wild ghosts escape from dreams. Each monster dances in the park.

3. Uv xroxne. Uv cvoz xroxne.

    Be afraid. Be very afraid.

Cryptogram #26
From Page 49

1. Tq Mwjjtvbbq, vtkombi otrb kdcb; vfjn hmtiki biowyb pdtr ndbwri. Bwom rtqikbd nwqobi fq kmb ywds.

    On Halloween, witches come true; wild ghosts escape from dreams. Each monster dances in the park.

2. C tgon yvby ck dntnrfbyckm Vbttginnk, in dbk mny tgly ck yvn abmcd gz abwn-rntcnon bku zbkyblh kg abyynf ivby bmn in bfn!

    I love that in celebrating Halloween, we can get lost in the magic of make-believe and fantasy no matter what age we are!

3. Nlftab, nlftab, plda qhn pmlftab. Odmb tfmh qhn gqfanmlh tfttab.

    Double, double, toil and trouble. Fire burn and cauldron bubble.

Cryptogram #27
From Page 50

1. Us uw ryws g oymxa tj atxyw etxyw!

    It is just a bunch of hocus pocus!

2. Soks ep tjs rckr noevo vkt cscwtkh hec.

    That is not dead which can eternal lie.

3. Dk obhogn. Dk qkhu obhogn.

    Be afraid. Be very afraid.

Cryptogram #28
From Page 51

1. Apakgwcg qm Tczzhlaad jhk c thkkhk jcd, la oemv uh ikcbg qd Hivhxak.

    Everyday is Halloween for a horror fan, we just go crazy in October.

2. Thpqmx, thpqmx, bhsm krt bfhpqmx. Usfx qpfr krt dkpmtfhr qpqqmx.

    Double, double, toil and trouble. Fire burn and cauldron bubble.

3. Xojybo, sywo pybo zo bkmof yalqo!

    Beware, take care he rides alone!

Cryptogram #29
From Page 52

1. Uah bapeue zgh szj stu uah pwh uazu ke tfgehj ke uah ahzjyhee apgehlzw.

   > The ghosts are bad but the one that is cursed is the headless horseman.

2. Zxtdt lxtdt ag mh afwiamwlahm, lxtdt ag mh xhddhd.

   > Where there is no imagination, there is no horror.

3. Jkdj qa ztj wndw lkquk udz njnbzdo oqn.

   > That is not dead which can eternal lie.

Cryptogram #30
From Page 53

1. Ejxmx gjxmx uy cf urdzucdgufc, gjxmx uy cf jfmmfm.

   > Where there is no imagination, there is no horror.

2. Lp Nxfflarrp, askvnrh vlgr kqcr; asfw dnlhkh rhvxzr jqlg wqrxgh. Rxvn glphkrq wxpvrh sp knr zxqt.

   > On Halloween, witches come true; wild ghosts escape from dreams. Each monster dances in the park.

3. Ur sypske. Ur brpx sypske.

   > Be afraid. Be very afraid.

Color Me In

www.ingramcontent.com/pod-product-compliance
Lightning Source LLC
LaVergne TN
LVHW060143080526
838202LV00049B/4066